BUSES IN LANCASHIRE

JOHN LAW

AMBERLEY

Typical of Ribble buses from the interwar period is VY 957, a 1929-built Leyland Lion PLSC3, now in preservation and seen in Blackpool on a wet weekend in October 1985. This vehicle today resides at Manchester's Museum of Transport.

First published 2019

Amberley Publishing
The Hill, Stroud
Gloucestershire, GL5 4EP

www.amberley-books.com

Copyright © John Law, 2019

The right of John Law to be identified as
the Author of this work has been asserted in
accordance with the Copyrights, Designs and
Patents Act 1988.

ISBN 978 1 4456 9551 8 (print)
ISBN 978 1 4456 9552 5 (ebook)

British Library Cataloguing in Publication Data.
A catalogue record for this book is available from
the British Library.

Origination by Amberley Publishing.
Printed in the UK.

Introduction

Today's Lancashire is a lot smaller than it used to be. Prior to 1974, it included Warrington (now lost to Cheshire), most of what is now known as Greater Manchester, the part of Merseyside north of the River Mersey and the Furness District. The latter was an exclave of Lancashire, since absorbed into Cumbria. A small compensation was gaining part of the Craven District (around Barnoldswick) from Yorkshire.

By coincidence, it was around 1974 that the author of this book first began visiting Lancashire on a regular basis to photograph the transport of the area.

Road transport in what is now Lancashire began in the usual way, with farmers converting horse-drawn carts into passenger carrying vehicles to get people into town on market days. In many English towns tramways began operating using horses as motive power but, with the exception of Preston, the presence of steep hills precluded this. Many of the East Lancashire towns introduced steam trams, while Lytham tried gas-powered cars, which were not successful and were replaced by horse cars.

One of the first towns to introduce electric traction to its tramways was Blackpool, with the first section opening in 1885. This seaside resort still operates electric trams today, with a coastal line running all the way from Starr Gate to Fleetwood. At the time of writing, an extension is under construction along Talbot Road to serve the town's main railway station.

Other than Blackpool, all of Lancashire's other municipal tram operations were electrified, but most were closed during the 1930s, with Blackburn Corporation's trams surviving until 1949. As trolleybuses were never employed, what is now Lancashire was served only by buses.

By 1974, after all the boundary changes, Lancashire was left with eight council-owned operations. Rawtenstall and Haslingden had been combined to form Rossendale, Accrington Corporation had become Hyndburn District Council and Lytham St Annes was renamed Fylde Borough Council.

The most northerly council-owned operation, Lancaster City Transport (itself combined with neighbouring Morecambe in 1974), went out of business in 1993, with Stagecoach taking over the depot, some vehicles and the services.

Burnley & Pendle Transport (formerly Burnley, Colne & Nelson) was also purchased by Stagecoach in 1996. The same fate befell Hyndburn Transport, again in 1996. Stagecoach later sold these operations to the Blazefield Group, now part of Transdev. Transdev later took over the bus services of Blackburn Transport in 2007. Recently, in 2018, Rossendale Transport also sold out to Transdev.

Fylde Borough Council survived until summer 1994, when it was bought by Blackpool Transport.

The former municipal operator Preston Borough Transport was sold to its employees in 1993 and remained in their hands until 2009, when the business was sold to Stagecoach. However, that year it passed to the Rotala Group due to the ensuing near monopoly.

These takeovers have now left Blackpool Transport as the only council-owned bus company in Lancashire and one of less than a dozen in the United Kingdom.

The whole of present-day Lancashire was also once the territory of Ribble Motor Services. Founded in 1919, it later became part of the British Electric Traction Group, absorbed by the National Bus Company (NBC) in 1969. The company's dark red livery was replaced during the early 1970s when NBC poppy red paintwork was applied.

In 1988 the Lancashire operations of Ribble were sold to a management buyout but purchased the following year by Stagecoach. However, in 2001, the company's East Lancashire operations were bought by the Blazefield Group, later passing to Transdev, making that company the largest bus company around Burnley, Accrington and Blackburn.

The independent sector was never very big in Lancashire, with one exception: J. Fishwick & Sons of Leyland, whose green buses could be seen in Preston and Chorley until the business ceased trading in 2015.

Deregulation in 1986 saw various small companies enter the stage carriage market, most having passed by the wayside. At the time of writing, Pilkington's of the Accrington area are the largest of the survivors.

Over the twentieth century the vehicles of Leyland Motors dominated the Lancashire bus scene, with a few notable exceptions; Blackburn's Guys and Burnley's Bristols, for example. Bodywork was often by one of two local manufacturers, East Lancs or Northern Counties, but not exclusively.

Today's offerings are very similar to those found elsewhere in the country, but still provide a great deal of variety and interest to any bus enthusiast.

Finally thanks to Jim Sambrooks and Bus Lists on the web with help in production of this publication.

Though this book is primarily concerned with buses, it would be churlish to ignore the trams still operated by Blackpool Transport. The fleet was modernised during the 1930s, deliveries including a batch of double-deck 'Balloon' cars built by English Electric in 1934 and the following year. A fine example is No. 701, looking very smart in red and white and seen on the Promenade in September 1993. The normal service along the 'Prom' is today maintained by the new Bombardier cars, but 701 has been retained as a heritage vehicle.

Blackpool Transport has long had a tradition of not throwing things away and, in the mid-1970s, rebuilt some 'Railcoaches' from the 1930s to become the 'One Man Operation' cars. One of them, No. 13, is seen in 1976, when fairly new, at Fleetwood terminus. They were not a great success and ten of the thirteen built were scrapped.

The Progress Twin Car sets were introduced by Blackpool Corporation between 1958 and 1960, the towing vehicles having been rebuilt from previous 'Railcoaches', while new trailers were constructed. In the summer of 2000, car 674 is seen dragging its trailer over the junction with the line to the main depot at Manchester Square.

Blackpool Transport maintains a sizeable fleet of heritage vehicle to operate over its tracks. One of the oldest is former Blackpool & Fleetwood Electric Tramway 'Box' car No. 40. Built in 1914, it is seen on a private hire job in July 1996, having just left the street-running section in Fleetwood town centre.

Naturally the Blackpool Transport bus fleet consisted mainly of Leyland buses, given the proximity of that manufacturer to the town. For many years fully fronted buses were favoured. One of the last of that design to be procured was 358 (YFR 358), a Leyland PD3/1 with seventy-three-seat Metro-Cammell bodywork, delivered new in 1962. It is seen, towards the end of its life, in the depot yard in 1977.

Half-cab Leylands later became the standard bus in the Blackpool fleet. A typical example is 534 (LFR 534F), a PD3A/1 with MCW bodywork seating seventy-one passengers. It was found outside Woolworth's store in St Annes-on-Sea sometime around 1974.

Blackpool Corporation Transport continued to order Leyland PD3A/1 vehicles virtually until production ceased in 1969. Delivered in August 1968 was 538 (LFR 538G), again with MCW H41/30R bodywork. It is seen amongst others of the breed in 1982, along with preserved Doncaster AEC Regal III No. 22, in the yard of Rigby Road depot, Blackpool Transport's main facility for both buses and trams.

Unusually, in the early 1990s, Blackpool turned to the AEC Swift to meet its single-deck requirements. Photographed sometime around 1975, outside Rigby Road depot is 552 (PFR 552H), delivered in 1970 with Marshall forty-seven-seat bodywork fitted with dual doorway.

Part of a later order of AEC Swifts, No. 566 (OFR 966M) was delivered in 1974 (again with a Marshall B47D body) to a newer design – a bit more pleasing to the eye in the author's opinion. It is seen parked close to Talbot Road bus station in Blackpool town centre in 1979.

With the close in production of Leyland half-cab double-deck buses, Blackpool Transport began to buy Leyland Atlanteans. A later example of this type, No. 305 (CBV 305S), an AN68A/2R with East Lancs bodywork seating eighty-six passengers, was photographed on the Promenade not long after delivery in 1977. An East Kent AEC Reliance/Duple coach is pursuing it.

Two more Blackpool 'standard' Leyland PD3A/1 buses, 540 (LFR 540G) and 503 (HFR 503E), rest in the yard of Rigby Road depot as late as October 1987. Alongside are two more recently acquired double-deck buses. They are 523 (627 DYE) and 526 (735 DYE), both ex-London Buses AEC Routemasters, originally numbered RM1627 and RM1735 respectively. Like other operators in the country, the fad for Routemasters did not last long.

In 1982 Blackpool Transport took delivery of a total of four unusual Dennis Dominator saloons with fifty-one seats and Marshall bodywork. One of them, No. 597 (VCW 597Y), was found behind the main works only a few days after its arrival. Only a few council-owned operators bought vehicles of this type.

Blackpool Transport was one of the last operators to receive Leyland Atlanteans. Built in 1984, No. 364 (B364 UBV) was an East Lancs-bodied AN68D/2R, fitted with seventy-eight coach seats. It was photographed at the foot of the town's famous Tower in October 1984.

The mid to late 1980s saw Blackpool Transport buy minibuses, in common with many other operators. Rather than the common panel van conversions (Ford Transit and Freight Rover Sherpas), a batch of VW LT55/Optare CityPacer nineteen seat vehicles was obtained. One of them, 550 (E550 GFR), is seen on Talbot Road in October 1987. The Bosley Arcade, seen behind the bus, was destroyed in a huge conflagration on February 2009, which also consumed the iconic Yates Wine Lodge.

With the demise of the Leyland Olympian, Blackpool Transport turned to its successor, the
Olympian, for its double-deck requirements. Volvo continued to produce this vehicle after taking
over the Lancashire firm. Fleet No. 378 (M378 SCK) was built by Volvo in 1994 and carried a
Northern Counties Palatine body with seventy-two seats. The date is the spring of 1996 and the
location is Talbot Road bus station, a gloomy affair that the cold winds from the Irish Sea were
funnelled through. Now closed, it is not missed.

Operating in a yellow and black 'Handybus' livery, Blackpool Transport's 271 (V271 HEC)
is seen beside the Tower in October 2001. This twenty-eight-seat Optare Solo was delivered
in 1999.

In recent times Blackpool Transport's fleet has been modernised and a fine new grey colour scheme has been adopted. It has been applied to No. 427 (SN17 MGZ), a smart Alexander Dennis E40D seventy-two-seat double-decker. It is seen travelling out of town along Poulton Road in the suburb of Hoohill, near Layton railway station, on 29 March 2017.

Also in the new livery is No. 557 (BG15 BTY), a Mercedes Benz Citaro thirty-eight-seat saloon, photographed on a wet 29 March 2017 on Talbot Road, close to the town's North railway station.

Formerly known as Lytham St Annes Corporation Transport, Fylde Borough Transport was created in 1974 and based in a depot in Squires Gate. The fleet of blue and white buses was used on a variety of routes serving the two hometowns and running into Blackpool itself. Seen in St Annes around 1974 is No. 55 (368 BTJ), a 1957-built Leyland Tiger Cub with locally built Burlingham bodywork, seating forty-four passengers.

Inside the Squires Gate depot, *c.* 1975, is Fylde Borough Transport 75 (ATD 279J). This Leyland Atlantean PDR1A/1 had bodywork by another Lancashire company – Northern Counties. It was capable of carrying seventy-seven seated passengers.

Photographed sometime around 1978 in St Annes town centre is Fylde Borough Transport 39 (HRN 106N), one of five Bristol RESL6L saloons. Each carried ECW bodywork fitted with forty-four dual-purpose seats. Note that, by this time, the full fleet name had been applied.

Fylde Borough Transport decided it was necessary to order a small batch of Duple Dominant coach-bodied Leyland Leopards. A total of seven were delivered, one of which, No. 35 (GCK 35S), was photographed on the outskirts of Lytham in 1978. Folding doors were fitted, making it suitable for stage carriage duties (and attracting a government grant), while passengers were provided with fifty-three comfortable seats.

In 1986 Fylde Borough Transport adopted the name Blue Buses and a new livery with two shades of blue. This is seen applied to No. 2 (H2 FBT), a DAF SB220 with Optare 'Delta' DP48F bodywork. It is seen in the Moor Park suburb of Preston in mid-1992 on a tendered working.

Having been an 'arm's length' company owned by Fylde Borough Council since 1986, the Blue Buses fleet was sold to its management in 1993, before being purchased by Blackpool Transport the following year. For just a couple of years, the Blue Buses operation was kept separate, though transfers were common between the two businesses. Illustrating that is a former Blackpool Transport Leyland Atlantean AN68A/2R with East Lancs bodywork, No. 325 (URN 325V). It was photographed beneath Blackpool Tower in spring 1996. Later that year, the blue livery vanished when the two companies were amalgamated.

The most northerly of Lancashire's council-owned bus operators to survive the 1974 boundary changes was Lancashire City Transport, which took over neighbouring Morecambe & Heysham Transport in that year. One of the most famous vehicles in the LCT fleet was No. 466 (NTF 466), a 1952-built Daimler CVG5 bodied by Northern Counties, seen in the main depot in October 1974. It was retained for transporting prisoners from the local penal establishments. 466 later entered preservation, retaining its old maroon LCT livery.

Lancashire City Transport No. 389 (389 JTD) was one of a pair of forty-three-seat Leyland Tiger Cubs, bodied by East Lancs and delivered in 1959. Still wearing its old livery, it was photographed in the yard at Morecambe in October 1974.

The fleet taken over from Morecambe & Heysham Transport consisted mainly of AEC types, including a sizeable number of Regent III double-deckers. One such, No. 79 (TTB 688), is seen passing The Battery in Morecambe, retaining its original colours, albeit with City of Lancaster fleet names, in October 1974. Like most of the others of its type, it has Park Royal bodywork.

By 1974, Morecambe & Heysham Transport had converted several of its Park Royal-bodied AEC Regent III buses to open-top. Rested up in Morecambe depot for the forthcoming winter was No. 62 (KTF 591), which had been delivered new in 1949.

Also seen inside Morecambe depot in October 1974 was No. 9 (UTJ 909H), which had been new to Morecambe & Heysham Transport. This Northern Counties-bodied AEC Swift was one of a trio delivered in 1970.

Lancaster City Council had become the fleet name adopted by mid-1979 when this photograph was taken in the city's bus station. The new blue livery is well illustrated, being applied to No. 206 (KTJ 206), one of three Leyland PD2/37 double-deckers with sixty-five-seat front-entrance East Lancs bodywork bought in 1965.

Lancaster City Transport, like many British operators, adopted minibus operation during the late 1980s and early 1990s. Seen at Lancaster bus station in mid-1991 is M11 (E404 BHK), a twenty-five-seat VW LT55/Optare City Pacer that had been new to Southend Borough Transport.

Another Optare product, a thirty-one-seat dual-purpose Metrorider, was one of the last vehicles delivered new to Lancaster City Transport in 1992. ML1 (K100 LCT) was photographed a few months after entering service at Lancaster bus station. In August 1993, Lancaster City Transport ceased trading, with Stagecoach taking over the services, the depot and the more modern vehicles.

Although Preston can trace its history back to Roman times, it was not until 2002 that it was granted city status. Even prior to that, Preston was an important large town and had a municipal bus fleet that was always full of interest. With the Leyland factory only a few miles down the road, it was natural for most of the vehicles to have been produced there. No. 49 (FRN 733) was no exception, being an all-Leyland PD2/10 fifty-six-seater, new in 1954. Twenty years later it is seen in front-line service, departing from the town's notable bus station.

Preston Corporation Transport liked their old Leyland PD2 types so much that they rebuilt some. No. 61 (originally registered FRN 740) was another 1954-built PD2/10, rebuilt in 1965 to become a PD3/6, with a Leyland body adapted by the Corporation to H38/32F layout, registered BCK 367C. As such it is seen in the bus station still in service in 1977.

In 1971 Preston purchased seven Leyland Panther saloons with dual-doored forty-eight-seat Seddon bodies. A further batch followed in 1972. The earliest one delivered, No. 223 (MCK 223J), was photographed in the bus station in 1976. Even in those days, some pedestrians preferred to risk life and limb crossing the bus running area, rather than braving the subway approach to the passenger terminal.

Unlike many operators, Preston took a liking to Leyland Panthers, to the extent that some second-hand ones were purchased. AUE 313J had been ordered by Warwickshire operator Stratford Blue but delivered to Midland Red. Totally non-standard in that fleet, it was soon disposed of to Preston, where it became No. 241. As such, with its dual-door Marshall body, it is seen in Preston bus station in 1977.

As well as the PD2 types, Preston also obtained a good number of the later and larger PD3s. Typical of the breed is this 1963-built PD3A/1 with seventy-seat Metro-Cammell bodywork. No. 90 (TRN 392) was photographed passing the railway station in 1976.

In later years Preston bought plenty of East Lancs-bodied Leyland Atlanteans, very much the standard type of double-decker for the area. A variation of the theme was No. 2 (DRN 2Y), an AN68D/2R, built as late as 1983. Carrying an East Lancs body fitted with eighty-four coach seats, it is seen on a normal service duty at Lower Penwortham terminus in the autumn of the year it was delivered.

For single-deck requirements Preston Bus turned to the Leyland Lynx, purchasing a total of fifteen. The later ones were built to dual-purpose standard, but the first two (10 and 11) had forty-seven bus seats. No. 11 (F211 YHG) is seen on a wet summer's day in 1989 departing from the bus station.

Preston Bus also bought a small number of Leyland Olympians, one of which, No. 135 (G35 OCK), was photographed in the bus station in spring 1996. Its Leyland-built body had a seating capacity of eighty-two, on high-backed coach seats.

Preston Bus was sold to its management in 1993. Under that umbrella a number of Optare Solo saloons were purchased, including No. 63 (PN52 ZVM). Dedicated to Park and Ride duties, this twenty-nine-seat vehicle is seen opposite the railway station entrance in September 2003.

Following a 'bus war' with Stagecoach, Preston Bus passed to that company in January 2009. However, later in that year, the Competition Commission ordered that Preston Bus be sold on. After a period of 'arm's length' operation by Stagecoach, the business passed to the Rotala Group in 2011. While under that ownership, No. 32305 (SK16 GXT), a Wright Streetlite WF, is departing from the iconic bus station on 23 March 2017.

Heading east out of Preston, the next major town reached is Blackburn. The Corporation here had been running buses since 1929. The year 1974 saw the fleet rebadged as Blackburn Borough Transport. Sometime around that year No. 150 (KBV 150) was photographed in the town's bus station, still in its old green livery. This bus is a 1958-built Guy Arab IV, bodied by local company East Lancs. Unlike most of the other Lancashire operators, Blackburn once had a liking for Guy buses. Note the Leyland Atlantean behind, newly painted in the green and red colour scheme.

In 1972 Blackburn received half a dozen Seddon RU saloons with East Lancs bodywork. Forty-five-seat bus No. 67 (SBV 67K) is seen parked in the bus station sometime around 1974.

As part of the 1974 local government reorganisation, Darwen Corporation Transport was taken over by its larger neighbour. Just after that, Blackburn Borough Transport No. 123 (WTB 167) was photographed in Blackburn. New to Darwen in 1955, this Leyland PD2/22 had an unusual Crossley fifty-six-seat body.

Blackburn Borough Transport 54 (ETF 484F), 58 (JTF 218F) and 56 (ETF 486F), from left to right, are seen in Darwen depot in early 1980. These three Leyland PD2 deckers had all been new to Darwen Corporation, but are seen here in Blackburn's new colours. Each bus has a sixty-five-seat East Lancs body, but 54 and 56 are of type PD2A/27, while 58 is a PD2/47.

Very much the standard bus of Blackburn Borough Transport in the 1970s, No. 84 (UBV 84L) is a Leyland Atlantean AN68/1R with eighty-six-seat East Lancs bodywork. It is photographed outside the railway station on a sunny day in mid-1979.

Another look inside Darwen depot in 1980. A most unusual bus is featured here, fleet No. 150 (LJF 5F). This ECW-bodied Bristol RESL6L had been purchased from Leicester City Transport.

In 1981, Blackburn Borough Transport bought a small batch of Dennis Dominator buses, with seventy-four-seat East Lancs bodies. No. 4 (DBV 4W) received a special livery to commemorate 100 years of public transport in the town and is seen here in Darwen town centre when almost new. (From an original slide in the author's collection)

Blackburn Borough Transport purchased both MCW and Optare Metrorider vehicles in relatively large numbers. A thirty-one-seat version of the latter, No. 628 (M628 WBV) was photographed in mid-1995 passing the railway station in the latest livery of the time.

Various colour schemes have been applied to the Blackburn Borough Transport fleet over the years. In October 2004, No. 12 (G289 UMJ) is seen in the latest version at Blackburn bus station. This Leyland Olympian with Leyland bodywork had been new to London Country (North West) in 1989.

A batch of five low-floor Dennis Tridents, bodied by East Lancs, turned out to be the last of the new buses bought by Blackburn Borough Transport. One of them, No. 3 (PN52 XKH), was found in Blackburn bus station on a sunny October day in 2004. The Blackburn Borough Transport operation passed to Transdev in 2007. Since then, the town's bus station has been rebuilt on a new site, further away from the railway station, but with far better facilities.

Accrington Corporation Transport became Borough of Hyndburn Transport in 1974, retaining the dark blue and red colour scheme. Still wearing its Accrington crest is fleet No. 154 (949 RTB), one of a pair of Leyland PD2/20 vehicles bought in 1960. Sixty-three-seat East Lancs bodywork is seen on this bus in the town centre *c.* 1974.

Most buses in Accrington terminated in a small and separate area next to the impressive Town Hall. Here, on a dull day sometime around 1974, is Hyndburn No. 169 (CTB 169E), having a layover between duties. This Leyland PD3A/2, bodied by East Lancs with seventy-two seats, was the last of a batch of five purchased in 1967.

Hyndburn No. 22 (KTC 335C) was one of just three Leyland Tiger Cub/East Lancs B43F saloons bought in 1965, though four similar vehicles had arrived a few years earlier. Again, we are in the town centre *c.* 1974/5.

Accrington's first Atlanteans appeared in 1969, with more appearing through the years up to 1978. No. 175 (CTC 175J) was a PDR1A/1 model of 1971, fitted with the inevitable East Lancs bodywork. This eighty-eight-seat bus is seen in Accrington town centre in 1981.

Accrington Corporation later settled on Bristols to fulfil its single-deck requirements. One of the first ones to enter the fleet was this RESL6G bodied by East Lancs. No. 27 (MTJ 927G), a forty-seven-seat saloon, is seen in Hyndburn days in Accrington in 1982.

In 1974/5, Borough of Hyndburn Transport received a further small batch of Bristol saloons. One of them, No. 40 (YTB 945N), an East Lancs-bodied RESL6G, with forty-two dual-purpose seats, is seen decorated for the Queen's Silver Jubilee in Accrington in 1977.

The year 1979 saw Hyndburn purchase a sole Dennis Dominator, bodied by East Lancs. No. 195 (VCW 195V) was captured on film in Accrington town centre in 1982. Several more Dominator/ East Lancs double-deckers appeared during the early 1980s.

Hyndburn also received two rare Dennis Falcon saloons, the second of which is pictured here in Accrington town centre in the spring of 1987. Forty coach seats were fitted inside the East Lancs bodywork of No. 51 (B51 XFV).

It was inevitable that the mid to late 1980s saw an influx of minibuses to the Hyndburn fleet. Most were bought new, but No. 21 (D511 NDA) had come from West Midlands PTE. This eighteen-seat Ford/Transit/Carlyle combination was photographed in Accrington in the spring of 1988. Note the 'Hy-Rider' branding.

Other than minibuses, the last vehicles purchased by Hyndburn were a number of Reebur-bodied Leyland Swifts. One of them, thirty-nine-seat vehicle No. 39 (H39 YCW), is seen in Accrington town centre in the early 1990s. In 1996, Borough of Hyndburn Transport was sold to the Stagecoach Group.

More 1974 political upheavals saw the towns of Burnley, Colne and Nelson pass control of the buses of that name to the newly formed Burnley & Pendle Transport (officially a 'Joint Transport Committee'). The BCN fleet name took quite a while to be phased out, as seen on page 37. The area was to see some of the UK's last half-cab single-deck vehicles in normal service, including No. 47 (DHG 47). This was one of fourteen Leyland PS2/14 saloons, fitted with thirty-nine-seat East Lancs bodywork, delivered between 1953 and 1955. This one was photographed in Burnley bus station in 1974.

Most of the half-cab saloons were withdrawn soon after the appearance of Burnley & Pendle, but No. 42 (CHG 542) got a new lease of life as a towing vehicle, and is seen at the main depot in Burnley around 1977.

Still lettered as a 'BCN' vehicle, Burnley & Pendle No. 54 (NHG 554) is seen in Burnley bus station sometime around 1975. This vehicle had been part of a batch of ten 1963-built Leyland Tiger Cubs. All were fitted with East Lancs forty-three-seat bodywork.

Although the Leyland PD3 in the background had received its new colours, Burnley & Pendle No. 74 (HHG 74F) remained in BCN livery when photographed at Burnley bus station *c.* 1975. One of several Leyland Panthers in the fleet, this one carried fifty-seat Northern Counties bodywork and had been delivered in 1968.

BCN received its first batch of Leyland National saloons in 1973, when five were delivered, each seating forty-four passengers. One of those first vehicles, No. 133 (VCW 133L), is seen in Burnley bus station, still in full BCN livery, *c.* 1975.

Burnley & Pendle owned a few Leyland Leopard/Duple Dominant coaches for private hire etc., but they were also able to be deployed on bus services by virtue of the 'grant aid'-type folding doors. No. 6 (SRN 6P) was photographed at the Queensgate depot in Burnley, not too long after delivery in 1976.

Showing the full colour version of the Burnley & Pendle livery for the first time within these pages, No. 116 (RHG 316K) is standing in a sunny Burnley bus station in 1979. This is one of a sizeable batch of Seddon-bodied Seddon Pennine RU forty-six seat saloons inherited from BCN.

Burnley & Pendle purchased several second-hand buses in the late 1970s. One was fleet No. 94 (JBR 100F), a Bristol RELL6G with Metro-Cammell bodywork, built to the specification of Sunderland Corporation. Originally a dual-doored vehicle, it is seen in B50F configuration, still in Tyne & Wear PTE livery, at Burnley bus station in 1978.

More Leyland Nationals appeared in the Burnley & Pendle fleet, including some of the later Mark 2 type in 1980. At first glance, No. 72 (FUH 32V) appears to be one of them, but the South Wales registration gives away the fact that this particular bus had come from Taff Ely District Council, Pontypridd. It is seen at Burnley bus station in August 1989.

Burnley & Pendle's first batch of double-deck buses to be bought new appeared in 1976 when fourteen Bristol VRT/SL3/6LXB types were delivered, bodied by East Lancs with seventy-five seats. No. 154 (URN 154R) looks splendid in its smart new livery at Padiham terminus in early 1978.

A further batch of Burnley & Pendle Bristol VRT/SL3/6LXB double-deckers arrived in 1978, this time with ECW bodies seating seventy-four passengers. Our example here is No. 168 (FFR 168S), photographed on a bright and sunny day at Burnley bus station in 1979.

After the discontinuation of the Leyland National types, Burnley & Pendle turned to Volvo and the B10M-55 chassis for their single-deck requirements. The first to be delivered, in 1988, with fifty-three-seat Alexander bodywork, No. 61 (E61 JFV) was found in Accrington when almost brand new.

Burnley & Pendle began to use 'Whizzard' branding for certain services in the mid-1990s. In spring 1994, No. 75 (K75 XCW) was photographed in Burnley bus station. This thirty-one-seat Optare Metrorider had been delivered the previous year.

Another Burnley & Pendle Volvo B10M-55 is seen here, in Colne, in spring 1994. No. 67 (G67 PFR), to add to the variety, carries East Lancs B51F bodywork.

More Volvo B10M-55 types appeared in 1990, this time with Alexander PS type bodywork, as seen on fifty-one-seat saloon No. 22 (H622 ACK). This fine vehicle is seen in Blackburn bus station, heading for Burnley and Rawtenstall.

To combat intense competition, Burnley & Pendle purchased five ex-London AEC Routemaster buses, each named after characters in the BBC soap opera *Eastenders*. Perhaps the most well liked of them was Dot Cotton, the moniker carried by fleet No. 187 (ALM 87B). New to London Transport as RM2987, this bus looks in fine fettle in Burnley bus station not too long before Burnley & Pendle sold out to the Stagecoach Group in 1997.

The municipal transport activities of Rawtenstall and Haslingden were merged to form the Rossendale Joint Transport Committee in 1968, but the 1974 local government reorganisation brought the two together and Rossendale Transport was born. Inherited from the former Rawtenstall fleet was No. 18 (RTC 822), an all-Leyland PD2/12 of 1953. It is seen in Accrington, *c.* 1974, on loan to Hyndburn Transport.

Another Rossendale bus on loan to neighbour, Hyndburn, was No. 64 (VTJ 735), a 1955-built Leyland PD2/20 with fifty-nine-seat East Lancs bodywork. Again, it is seen in Accrington *c.* 1974.

A typical saloon in the Rossendale fleet, No. 1 (WTJ 901L) is seen inside the main depot in Rawtenstall in summer 1979. This was one of five Leyland Leopard/East Lancs forty-five-seat saloons bought in 1973. Further single-deck vehicles followed, but with chassis built by Bristol.

Rossendale also made use of double-deck buses, as illustrated by this 1982 view of No. 46 (DTJ 960E), taken in Accrington. This Leyland PD3/14 with East Lancs bodywork had been new to Haslingden Corporation in 1967.

The years between 1977 and 1982 saw Rossendale take in several small batches of Leyland Atlantean-type double-deck buses. Included in the 1978 intake was No. 18 (STE 18S), an AN68/1R with seventy-five-seat East Lancs bodywork. It was photographed in Accrington in 1981.

An unusual second-hand purchase by Rossendale was No. 30 (JUS 795N), one of three ex-Strathclyde PTE Leyland Atlanteans (this one being an AN68/1R), bodied by Alexander. It is seen inside Rawtenstall depot in 1987, advertising the local brew from Blackburn.

Another vehicle to enter the Rossendale fleet from a previous operator was No. 32 (B102 PHC). This coach-seated Leyland Olympian, bodied by East Lancs, had been new to Eastbourne buses. After service with Rossendale, it went on to serve the good people of Staffordshire with Stevenson's of Spath.

No. 29 (M529 RHG) in the Rossendale fleet was bought new in 1994. This Volvo Olympian with seventy-two-seat Alexander Royale bodywork was photographed in Rawtenstall town centre in mid-1995.

By 1998 (the date of this photograph) the low-floor saloon had arrived in the Rossendale fleet. No. 115 (S115 KRN), a Dennis Dart SPD/Plaxton forty-seat bus, was captured on film in central Rawtenstall.

In its last years Rossendale Transport rebranded itself as 'Rosso', well displayed on No. 124 (LF52 USY), one of ten Wight Eclipse-bodied Volvo B7TL types acquired second-hand. This particular one had been new to Arriva in London, originally with a two-door layout. It was photographed in Accrington on 27 March 2017. Later that year Rossendale Council approved the sale of the bus operations and Transdev took over early in 2018.

Ribble Motor Services could trace its history back to 1919. It later became part of the British Electric Traction Group, and then passed to the National Bus Company, where it was allocated the poppy red livery. In this 1974 photograph, at Blackpool depot yard, all four buses have received the new colours. On the left is No. 1664 (NTN 564), a lowbridge Leyland Atlantean PDR1/1. Alongside is something rarer, No. 1978 (MCK 371), a Burlingham-bodied Leyland PD3/1 that had come from Scout Motor Services, a company acquired in 1961 and finally absorbed in 1968. Two of the many fully fronted Leyland PD3/4 types make up the quartet.

In 1964/5, Ribble bought a small batch of rather unusual double-deckers. One of them, No. 1860 (UCK 860), an Albion Lowlander with full front Alexander bodywork seating seventy-two passengers, is seen in Preston bus station *c.* 1974.

The fully fronted Leyland Titan PD3 types became the standard double-deck vehicle in the Ribble fleet during the early 1960s, lasting into the NBC era. Here we have No. 1742 (PCK 383), a PD3/5 of 1961, with Metro-Cammell seventy-two-seat bodywork, photographed in Blackburn *c.* 1975.

Seen in its bright livery, identical No. 1729 (PCK 370) was photographed ascending Fishergate Hill into Preston town centre, passing County Hall, as late as 1981.

Like many NBC operators, Ribble Motor Services took in plenty of Leyland Nationals to satisfy the company's single-deck requirements. Here is one, No. 454 (NTC 634M), a forty-nine-seat example, seen in Preston bus station in 1974 not long after it was delivered.

Despite its proximity to the Leyland factory and its liking for such vehicles, Ribble also bought a good number of Bristol RESL6L saloons between 1970 and 1972. Marshall bodied the earlier ones, but the 1971 and 1972 batches received forty-seven-seat ECW bodies. Here is No. 360 (OCK 360K) loading up in Burnley bus station.

Ribble also bought plenty of Leyland Leopards, in the form of buses, coaches and dual-purpose vehicles. One of the latter, No. 892 (ECK 892E), with forty-nine-seat Marshall bodywork, is seen in Lancaster bus station, *c.* 1979.

As well as lowbridge PDR1/1 Leyland Atlanteans, Ribble also bought a medium sized batch of normal height examples. Here is No. 1696 (NRN 586), delivered in 1960, with Metro-Cammell seventy-seven-seat bodywork. Fishergate Hill, Preston, 1981.

In 1971/2, Ribble also took in twenty or so Bristol VRT/SL6G double-deck buses with seventy-seat ECW bodies, built to the earliest design for this type. No. 1987 (OCK 987K) was photographed speeding past the hotels on Fishergate Hill, Preston, in 1981.

Ribble No. 1015 (PTF 710L), a Bristol RELH6L with ECW C49F bodywork, is seen here in Preston bus station in NBC dual-purpose livery.

Another Ribble coach in dual-purpose colours, No. 1091 (YFR 491R), was found in Blackburn bus station when new in 1977. It is a Leyland Leopard with Duple Dominant forty-seven-seat bodywork, fitted with folding doors to make it suitable for stage carriage work and attracting a government grant.

An earlier Leyland Leopard coach, No. 958 (HRN 958G), was photographed at Blackpool coach station in 1982 wearing National Express white paintwork. Forty-nine-seat Plaxton Elite bodywork is featured.

Between 1973 and 1976, Ribble Motor Services received a huge batch of Leyland Atlantean AN68/1R double-deck buses. The later ones were bodied by ECW, but No. 1324 (RTF 635M) carried a Park Royal seventy-three-seat body. It is seen at Blackpool coach station, with Rigby Road tram depot behind, *c*. 1976.

Ribble bought plenty of Leyland National 2 saloons in the late 1970s and early 1980s. One of them, No. 831 (DBV 831W) a forty-four-seater delivered in August 1980, was photographed in the autumn sun in Fleetwood *c*. 1981.

Ribble only bought two Bristol LHS6L vehicles, one of which is seen on a dull day in Burnley in 1984. Branded as 'Betty's Bus', for a community service in the rural Ribble Valley, No. 272 (FBV 272W) has ECW thirty-five-seat bodywork.

Contrasting with the above picture, it is a nice sunny day in Morecambe in 1979 and Ribble had plenty of vehicles like this. No. 1445 (LHG 445T), almost new when photographed, is an ECW-bodied Bristol VRT/SL3/501.

It is November 1986 and Ribble has acquired a rare second-hand double-deck bus. No. 1624 (JFR 396N), a Leyland Atlantean AN68/1R bodied by East Lancs, had been new to Blackburn Transport. It is seen in Fishergate, Preston, passing the long-closed Theatre Hotel, a cracking Boddington's house back then.

Seen in 1987, showing the new livery of the time, is No. 901 (C544 RAO), a Leyland Lynx saloon. Destined to remain unique in the Ribble fleet, it had started life as a pre-production demonstrator with Leyland Motors. The location is Blackburn bus station.

In a special colour scheme for express services, Ribble No. 2173 (C173 ECK) is pictured leaving Preston bus station for Liverpool in autumn 1988. One of many ECW-bodied Leyland Olympians in the fleet, this one could fit seventy-two passengers into comfortable coach seats.

The year 1986 saw the introduction of deregulation and many operators purchased tiny minibuses to help combat competition. Ribble was no exception. Here we have Freight Rover Sherpa/Dormobile sixteen-seater No. 578 (D578 VBV) at Blackburn in spring 1987. Two years later, Ribble Motor Services passed to the Stagecoach Group.

As well as the vehicles of Ribble Motor Services, those of Barrow Borough Transport also passed to Stagecoach. Inherited from the latter concern was No. 756 (NEO 832R), a forty-nine-seat Leyland National. It is seen in sunny Morecambe in mid-1991.

Once unique in the Ribble fleet, Stagecoach No. 900 (B900 WRN) was a Duple Dominant-bodied Leyland Tiger forty-nine-seat bus. It was photographed in Lancaster bus station in mid-1991. After sale by Stagecoach the vehicle entered preservation.

As mentioned earlier, Lancaster City Transport routes and some vehicles passed to Stagecoach in 1993. In October of that year Stagecoach Ribble No. 1214 (A214 MCK), which had been new to Lancaster, was found in Preston bus station still wearing its old colours. This Leyland Atlantean AN68D/2R with bodywork by East Lancs had been constructed in 1984.

Another unusual bus in the Stagecoach Ribble fleet, No. 1135 (F135 SPX) was photographed in Lancaster bus station in the summer of 1992. This Dennis Javelin/Duple 300 had been transferred from Hampshire, where it had borne the name *King Arthur*. This bus has since been preserved.

Another wet day! It is the summer of 1989 and Stagecoach Ribble No. 1449 (LEO 734Y) is seen departing from Preston bus station on a local run to Penwortham. This Leyland Atlantean AN68D/1R had been new to Barrow Borough Transport as No. 104. Northern Counties seventy-five-seat bodywork is carried.

Stagecoach Ribble Optare Metrorider 450 (K450 YCW) is seen in an advertising livery in Lancaster in spring 1996. This thirty-one-seat bus had been new to Lancaster City Transport as No. ML2 (K200 LCT) in 1992.

Another second-hand vehicle in the Stagecoach Ribble fleet. Type 2 Leyland National No. 905 (MDS 866V) had been transferred from the Scottish operations. It had originally been new to Central SMT. With competition from M & M Coaches to the rear, it is seen in Accrington in the summer of 2000.

With 'Zippy' branding, Stagecoach Ribble No. 615 (D615 BCX) was found operating in Chorley on a wet day in 1991. This minibus, new in 1987, was an Iveco/Fiat 49.10 bodied by Robin Hood and fitted with just twenty-one seats.

It is September 2002 and the sun is shining over Blackburn. Stagecoach No. 653 (N462 VOD) looks smart in the latest livery as it heads for Chorley. It is a twenty-three-seat Mercedes 709D/ Alexander minibus. Despite the Devon registration, this vehicle had been new to Ribble operations.

Today Stagecoach has a much smaller presence in Lancashire, but still retains an important role. Seen in Chorley on a Stagecoach Gold service to Bolton on 30 March 2017 is No. 15242 (YN65 XET). This Scania N23OUD, bodied by Alexander, had been supplied new for the Liverpool area operations.

Prior to deregulation, the southern part of the Ribble business was split off to form the reinvented North Western Road Car Company. The firm's vehicles could be found in a few places in Lancashire, including Blackburn, where No. 398 (OCK 370K) was photographed in autumn 1988. This Bristol RESL6L/ECW saloon had been new to Ribble as No. 370 in 1972.

North Western was sold to the Drawlane Group in 1988, later to become British Bus. Under Drawlane ownership we see 640 (G640 CHF) heading for Liverpool as it passes Preston railway station in mid-1990. New to North Western late in the previous year, it is an East Lancs-bodied Volvo B10M-50, capable of seating eighty-eight passengers.

In 1996, British Bus was acquired by the Cowie Group, which later changed its name to Arriva. A former North Western East Lancs-bodied Volvo B10M-50, No. 646 (G661 DTJ) was photographed in central Ormskirk in the summer of 2000.

Some of Arriva's frequent and prestigious services are branded as 'Sapphire', including the Bolton–Wigan–Chorley route. Most of this is, of course, within Greater Manchester, but the northern end, the historic town of Chorley, has remained within Lancashire. In that town, within a few yards of the end of its long journey, we see No. 2685 (CX58 EVG) – a Wright-bodied VDL DE02 – on 30 March 2017. At the time of writing, Germany's Deutsche Bahn owns Arriva.

April 2001 saw the Stagecoach operations in East Lancashire move to the Blazefield Group. Only a couple of months later No. 701 (W701 BFV) was photographed in Accrington, still wearing its stripes but labelled as a Lancashire United vehicle. By this time, Blazefield had split its new operations into two: Lancashire United and Burnley & Pendle. For the record the vehicle is a Dennis Dart SLF/Plaxton B29F.

Proudly showing off its new Burnley & Pendle colours, No. 664 (M384 VWX) was photographed in central Burnley in summer 2002. This Alexander-bodied Volvo B6-50 had been transferred from another Blazefield company, Harrogate & District.

Burnley & Pendle No. 453 (M453 VCW) had been inherited from the Stagecoach Ribble fleet. Very much a standard vehicle of the time, it was a Volvo B10M-53 with Alexander PS type bodywork, to dual-purpose specification. It was photographed in Burnley bus station in the summer of 2002.

No. 2712 (Y712 HRN) was photographed, again in summer 2002, at Colne bus station, in a dedicated livery for the X43 service to Manchester. New in the previous year, this Plaxton-bodied Volvo B7TL was fitted with coach seating for such long-distance journeys.

Transfers were fairly common within the Blazefield Group. No. 926 (P426 UUG), a coach-seated Volvo Olympian/Alexander Royale, had started life with Yorkshire Coastliner but is seen with Lancashire United fleet names in Burnley in October 2004.

Also in Lancashire United livery, No. 2178 (C178 ECK), an ex-Ribble Leyland Olympian/ECW with coach seats, is seen on a non-passenger working in Blackburn in October 2004.

In January 2006 the Blazefield operations in East Lancashire were transferred to Transdev, bringing smart new liveries to the area. On 27 March 2017, No. 1102 (PN02 HVJ) was photographed in Blackburn as a Lancashire United bus. This Volvo B10BLE has forty-four-seat Wright bodywork.

Transdev Burnley & Pendle Optare Versa saloon No. 256 (YJ57 XVT), branded for 'Starship' services, was photographed on Accrington Road in Burnley on 25 July 2009. It is passing the Alma Inn, still open then – but now sadly closed.

Another Optare Versa, No. 234 (YJ16 DVZ), is seen in the vicinity of Blackburn's new bus station on 27 March 2017. As can be seen, local services here are being branded as 'The Blackburn Bus Company'.

Transdev's Blackburn–Accrington–Manchester route, known as the 'redEXPRESS' has dedicated vehicles, one of which – No. 3602 (X2 VTD) – is seen arriving at Accrington bus station on 27 March 2017. Re-registered from YC53 MXN, this coach-seated Volvo B7TL/Wright had originated with Harrogate & District.

The municipal operators of the Halifax area once ran into Burnley. Former Calderdale Joint Omnibus Committee Daimler Fleetline/Northern Counties RCP 278K, seen as West Yorkshire PTE No. 3298, was photographed in Burnley bus station in the mid-1970s. Today First Bus operates the route.

In the 1970s National Travel North West was formed to take care of express services in the area. Later it became National Travel West, as seen on No. N76 (SJA 406K). This coach-seated Leyland Leopard/Alexander Y type had been new to the original North Western Road Car Company. It was photographed at Blackpool coach station *c.* 1981.

J. Fishwick & Sons of Leyland operated frequent services along the Preston–Leyland–Chorley
corridor. Naturally, it was common for Leyland-built buses to be bought for these duties,
including ones that had been previously employed as demonstrator vehicles for Leyland Motors.
Fishwick's No. 1 (JTJ 667F), a Park Royal-bodied Leyland Panther, is a good example, seen in
Preston bus station *c.* 1975.

Three of Fishwick's lowbridge Weymann-bodied Leyland PDR1/1 Atlanteans, Nos 35 (TTE
643D), 26 (TTE 642D), and 25 (TTE 641D), are seen towards the end of their lives in the depot
yard in February 1980.

Fishwick's did not just buy Leylands. Here is a rare single-deck, rear-engined, Daimler Fleetline. The bodywork was built by Fishwick's themselves, under the Fowler brand. No. 7 (TTJ 496M) was photographed passing Preston railway station at speed in 1978.

J. Fishwick & Sons also operated coaches in a different livery to the service buses. One of them, a Duple Northern-bodied Leyland Leopard forty-nine-seat vehicle, No. C1 (RTD 432C), is seen in the main depot in January 1976.

The rather angular looking Fowler bodywork, seating forty-four passengers, is fitted onto a Leyland Leopard chassis. Fishwick's No. 27 (BTD 780J), one of three received in 1970, is seen at the depot *c.* 1980.

Another example of Fowler bodywork, again capable of seating forty-four passengers, this time on a Leyland Tiger Cub chassis. No. 12 (VTD 441H) was photographed leaving Preston bus station on a short working to the Queens Hotel in Leyland *c.* 1975.

Fishwick's No. 22 (SRN 103P), an East Lancs-bodied Leyland Atlantean AN68/1R bought new in 1976, is seen on Fishergate in Preston not long after delivery. The Queens pub it is passing has long since closed.

Leyland Titan B15 prototype FHG 592S began life as a demonstrator with Leyland Motors. By the time of this photograph (*c.* 1981) it had passed to Fishwick's on long-term loan, but retained its originally livery. Given fleet No. 20, the Park Royal-bodied bus is seen at the depot.

In the early 1980s Fishwick's standardised on the Leyland National 2 as its standard saloon. Almost new No. 7 (GCK 428W), a forty-nine-seat bus, was photographed on a sunny Fishergate in Preston in 1981.

J. Fishwick & Sons continued with Leyland-built buses as long as possible. One of the last ones bought was No. 5 (H65 CCK), a fifty-one-seat Leyland Lynx 2. It is seen parked at Preston bus station in October 1994. Sadly, J. Fishwick & Sons ceased trading in 2015 and most bus services in the area are now in the hands of Stagecoach.

Blue Bus once operated many services in the Wigan area, with an occasional foray into Lancashire. Seen in September 2003, passing the excellent Old Vic pub beside Preston station, is No. 33 (V33 BLU). This East Lancs-bodied DAF SB220 forty-two-seat bus was delivered in 2000. Blue Bus lasted until 2005, when Arriva took over.

Several small operators have been known to run minibuses on services in the Blackburn and Darwen area, including J & S Travel of Darwen. JST 160N, a personalised registration for the operator, means that it has proved impossible to ascertain full details of this Mercedes/Plaxton Beaver. It is seen at its Darwen terminus in October 2004, with the town hall behind.

Darwen Coach Services also employed minibuses in the area in those years after deregulation. On service in Blackburn in mid-1995 was D181 NON. This Freight Rover Sherpa/Carlyle eighteen-seater had started life with Manchester Minibuses in 1987.

Perhaps more suited to public service operation was Darwen Coach Services F917 YWY, a Mercedes 811D/Optare StarRider. As a twenty-six-seat bus, it had previously seen service with London Transport as No. SR17. It is seen at Blackburn bus station in October 2004.

A lot of the work done by Lonsdale Coaches of Morecambe was transporting workers to and from the nuclear power plant at Heysham. Engaged on such duties on a damp day in 1981 is UTD 285H, painted in all over orange. This unusual Bristol LH6L/Northern Counties saloon had started life with Lancashire United in 1969. The location is close to the Battery in Morecambe and it is pleasant to report that the Cumberland View pub in the background is still selling Thwaite's Beers.

Heysham Travel did similar work to Lonsdale Coaches, but later branched out into stage carriage work. Operating a local route in Lancaster in 1996 is GSG 127T. This Leyland Leopard/Duple Dominant coach had been new to Alexander (Fife) where it had carried fleet No. FPE127. By the date of this photograph Heysham Travel was owned by MTL of Liverpool, who later sold the business to Stagecoach.

Clitheroe-based Lakeland Coaches is today a well-respected business operating tours and contract work. At one time, it also undertook stage carriage work, with one route even reaching Skipton. Awaiting duty by Clitheroe railway station in mid-1995 is L893 KCK, a Mercedes 711D/Plaxton twenty-five-seat minibus branded for the 'Village Express' service.

Border Buses was an operator in the Burnley area that came to prominence in the latter half of the 1990s. Seen in Burnley in mid-1995 is ABN 721V, an East Lancs-bodied Leyland Atlantean AN68A/1R that had previously been No. 21 in the Rossendale fleet.

Operating the Colne town service in 1998 is H105 MOB, owned by Border Buses. This small Dennis Dart/Carlyle bus, originally a twenty-eight-seater, had been new to London Buses as DT105.

By the summer of 2000, when this photograph was taken, Border Buses was owned by the Status Group and was just about to be taken over by Northern Blue (see page 85). Operating an express service is No. 475 (XUX 275Y), a Duple Dominant-bodied Leyland Tiger seen at its Fleetwood terminus.

M & M Coaches of Accrington began competitive services around the East Lancashire towns after deregulation, even adopting the old Accrington Corporation colours. These have been applied to Dodge S56/Northern Counties minibus E170 AUX, seen in Accrington in the summer of 2000. M & M ceased to exist in 2016.

Mercers/Premier of Longridge (a small town north-east of Preston) was a long established coach business. As well as the usual private hire and tours, some contract work was undertaken and NTV 735M was used on these duties. This dual-doored Leyland National had previously been No. 735 in the Nottingham City Transport fleet. It is seen in the depot yard in late 1984.

After deregulation Mercers decided to enter the stage carriage market and NTV 735M (see previous page) was repainted for such work. It was photographed on a local service in Preston bus station in 1986.

Mercers also used double-deck buses on their route, including OJD 222R, which was found having a rest in the parking area of Preston bus station in autumn 1988. Formerly known as DMS2222 in the London Buses fleet, it is a Leyland Fleetline bodied by MCW to London's standard design. Mercers later gave up stage carriage work and the company no longer exists.

Lancashire Rose was a short-lived operator that ran a few services in and around Preston. Departing from the bus station for the suburb of Farringdon Park in mid-1995 is C810 CBU. This Dodge S56/Northern Counties eighteen-seat minibus had been new to Greater Manchester Transport.

Fylde independent Phoenix of Cleveleys dabbled in the stage carriage market by winning tendered work from the local councils. On such a duty in September 1996, at Lancaster bus station, is N295 DWE. New to the company earlier that year, the vehicle is a Mercedes 811D with Mellor thirty-one-seat bodywork.

Northern Blue began operating in 1999 and soon became a major force in the bus scene of the East Lancashire towns. A good variety of vehicles were owned including No. 2 (RJI 6862). Originally a Leyland National registered MCA 677T with Crosville, East Lancashire Coachbuilders had converted it to Greenway specifications for Crosville Wales. It was photographed in Burnley in summer 2002.

This Mercedes 709D minibus, with Dormobile-built twenty-nine-seat body, No. 94 (G94 ERP), had been new to Milton Keynes Citybus in 1989. By summer 2002 it had passed to Northern Blue and was found in Colne's tiny bus station.

Photographed on a local service to Nelson at Burnley bus station in October 2004 is R233 SCH. This thirty-one-seat Optare Metrorider had come to Northern Blue from Nottingham City Transport.

On the same sunny October day at Burnley bus station we see Northern Blue No. 145 (B45 NDX). New in 1985 as a dual-doored Leyland Olympian/East Lancs double-decker with Ipswich Buses, it was later converted to single-door. Northern Blue survived as an independent until 2007, when Transdev took over.

Tyrers is a coach firm founded in Adlington, Lancashire, in 1972. Today the business has moved to Chorley and has around eighty vehicles. A small amount of bus service work is still undertaken, but not as much as during the period after regulation. Back in October 1987, we see OAH 552M waiting to depart from Burnley bus station for Barnoldswick. This Leyland National had been delivered new to Eastern Counties as LN552.

Though Tyrers own some smart double-deck buses, these are normally confined to student duties. Stage services tend to be run by mini/midi buses. Found in Burnley town centre, on Manchester Road, in summer 2002 was J946 JJR. This twenty-six-seat Optare Metrorider had come from the Go Ahead Group's North East operation.

One of several operators to compete on the Hyndburn circular route, Accrington Coachways had an interesting fleet. Not totally suitable for stage carriage duties was MJX 808T, photographed in Blackburn bus station in the spring of 1987. This Caetano-bodied fifty-six-seat Ford R1114 coach had started life with a Yorkshire operator in Bradford.

By the time of this photograph, spring 1988, a 'proper' bus was in use on local service duties. OGM 604M, a Leyland Leopard with Alexander 'Y' type bodywork, is soon to load up in Accrington. This vehicle had been originally delivered to Central SMT in Scotland. Accrington Coachways is no longer trading.

Pilkington's started running stage services in those mad years after deregulation. This operation is still in business today, with several routes centred on Accrington. In mid-1995 Leyland National PIB 6945 was photographed in Blackburn, heading back to its home town. This vehicle, originally registered GVV 888N, had been new as a forty-nine-seat bus with United Counties, where it carried fleet No. 497.

Today's legislation means that low-floor buses are mandatory for stage carriage work and the Pilkington business is no exception. Looking very smart in the sun on 27 March 2017 is R14 PLK, arriving at Accrington's brand new bus station. This DAF DB250, with bodywork by Alexander, had been new to Arriva in London, where it had borne fleet No. DLA172 and registration W372 VGJ.

Powercrafts was another small operator to be found in the busy Blackburn/Accrington area. Found in Blackburn in spring 1988 was GLS 280N. This Leyland Leopard/Alexander Y type fifty-three-seat saloon had been new to Alexander (Midland) in Scotland.

Pennine Motor Services, a North Yorkshire operator based at Gargrave, once ran all the way from Skipton to Lancaster. Sometime around 1978, we see RWY 378M having just left Lancaster bus station and heading back home. This 1974-built Leyland Leopard with Plaxton Elite Express forty-nine-seat coachwork was, at the time, ideal for such a journey. After deregulation, Pennine Motor Services also began services into Burnley, but has since ceased trading.

Catch 22 Bus is a relative newcomer to the stage carriage scene of the Fylde Peninsula. Based in Mereside, Blackpool, a smart fleet of saloons is owned. Seen in central Blackpool on 29 March 2017 is W466 UAG, a Dennis Dart SLF/Plaxton that had been new to East Yorkshire Motor Services.

Cranberry Coachways, still in business at the time of writing, once ran a few tendered services in the Blackburn area. In the summer of 2000, one of the company's minibuses was found in Blackburn bus station, heading for the village of Guide, a few miles to the south. This Mercedes minibus, registered G481 HNP, had previously seen service with Bullock's of Greater Manchester. By 2002 it had been re-registered as BNZ 5830 but has since been scrapped.

A small firm called C & H Coaches of Fleetwood once ran a service between Lancaster and Knott End. Operating such a duty in early 1992 is ex-Eastern Counties JCL 811V. This Willowbrook-bodied Leyland Leopard coach was photographed in Lancaster, just outside the bus station.

Merseyside independent ABC Travel once ran several services in Lancashire and beyond. Seen in the outskirts of Leyland is BPY 401T, a Leyland Leopard/Duple Dominant coach that had been new to Cleveland Transit as fleet No. S401. ABC Travel later passed to CMT, another Merseyside operator.

Town Midi Coaches was a small operator in the 1990s, running a few services around the East Lancashire towns. Photographed in Clitheroe in the summer of 1995 is Freight Rover Sherpa D108 NOJ. This eighteen-seat minibus, adopted for PSV use by Carlyle, had been new to Manchester Minibuses. Sadly, the Victoria pub, a prominent feature of Clitheroe town centre, is no longer with us.

New in 1989 to Welsh operator Williams of Llanberis, G772 FJC is a VW LT55/Opare City Pacer twenty-five-seat bus. It is seen here in Accrington in spring 1994, in the hands of Town Midi Coaches.

Chorley-based Reeves Coach Hire, still in business today, once gained the contract to run the infrequent former Ribble 259 route from Blackburn to Chorley. Seen on such a duty in Blackburn bus station in mid-1990 is Bedford YRQ/Plaxton coach HPG 329N. It had been new to Buckinghamshire operator Jeffways & Pilot of High Wycombe.

Ellen Smith was a well-respected Rochdale operator that ran regular express services to the Lancashire coast. The company's coaches always featured the leaping tiger logo, which can be seen halfway along this Plaxton Elite-bodied Leyland Leopard, registered PDK 763H. It was captured on film in Lancaster bus station operating the X50 service to Morecambe in 1982.

Another firm operated express services to the coast, mainly during the 1990s. East Lancashire's SRU 146R is seen in Blackburn in mid-1995, pausing while en route to Morecambe on route 100. This Leyland Leopard with Plaxton Supreme Express coachwork had been new as a forty-nine-seat vehicle to Hants & Dorset Motor Services.

A & A Coaches was a small business based in a yard at Accrington. The company specialised in private hire and schools duties, the latter being the reason for the purchase of 91 HBC. Seen at the company's headquarters in 1982, this 1964-built Leyland PD3A/1 with East Lancs bodywork had been new to Leicester City Transport.

Another operator from East Lancashire, Ribblesdale of Blackburn, were the owners of this rather unusual AEC Reliance coach with Caetano bodywork, registered XTH 944M. It had been new to Welsh independent Eynon's of Trimsaran, who had used it on stage carriage duties (hence the folding doors). It is seen at Blackpool coach station in 1981.

An unusual vehicle to finish this book on buses in Lancashire is the short-lived steam bus operation in Clitheroe. KG 1123 had been new as a flat-bed Sentinel steam lorry in 1932, only later being fitted with a thirty-two-seat wooden body. In the company of a Transdev Lancashire United Volvo/Wright saloon, it is seen at Clitheroe Interchange in summer 2009. (Jim Sambrooks)